Table of Contents

D1197893

Timeline

1986: Aubrey Drake Graham is born.

1991: Aubrey's parents divorce.

1999: Aubrey celebrates his bar mitzvah.

2001: Aubrey is cast as Jimmy Brooks in *Degrassi: The Next Generation.*

2006: Aubrey releases his first mixtape, *Room for Improvement,* using the name Drake.

2007: Drake releases his second mixtape, *Comeback Season.*

2008: Drake is fired from *Degrassi: The Next Generation.*

Drake meets Lil Wayne, who becomes his mentor.

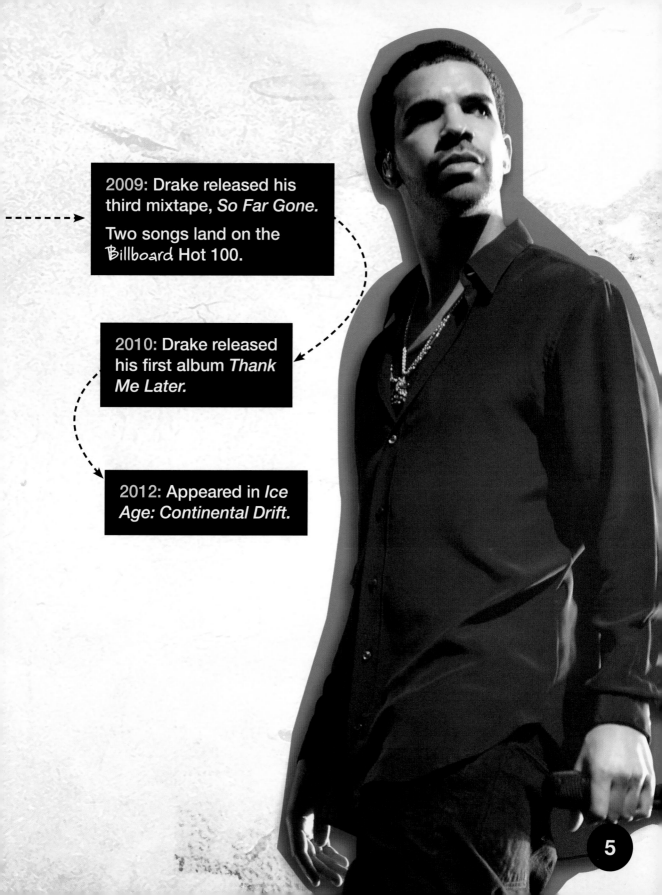

2009: Drake released his third mixtape, *So Far Gone.*

Two songs land on the Billboard Hot 100.

2010: Drake released his first album *Thank Me Later.*

2012: Appeared in *Ice Age: Continental Drift.*

5

Aubrey's Early Life

Many people dream of becoming a famous actor or singer. Few people are able to live out those dreams. Even fewer are able to do both. Drake is one of those rare people.

Aubrey Drake Graham was born on October 24, 1986. His mother is white, Jewish, and lives in Canada. Aubrey's father is an African American Catholic from Memphis, Tennessee. He was a drummer who performed with famous musicians. Aubrey's parents had such different lives that their marriage was difficult. Finally, when he was in preschool, Aubrey's parents divorced.

Aubrey lived with his mother in Toronto. They had a home in a wealthy Jewish neighborhood. His mother taught school to support them.

Aubrey's father rarely visited him when he was young. He used drugs, which made him undependable at times. Aubrey's father also spent some time in jail. Aubrey missed his father, but learned not to count on him. As an adult Aubrey recalled, "I spent too many nights looking by the window, seeing if the car was going to pull up. And the car never came."

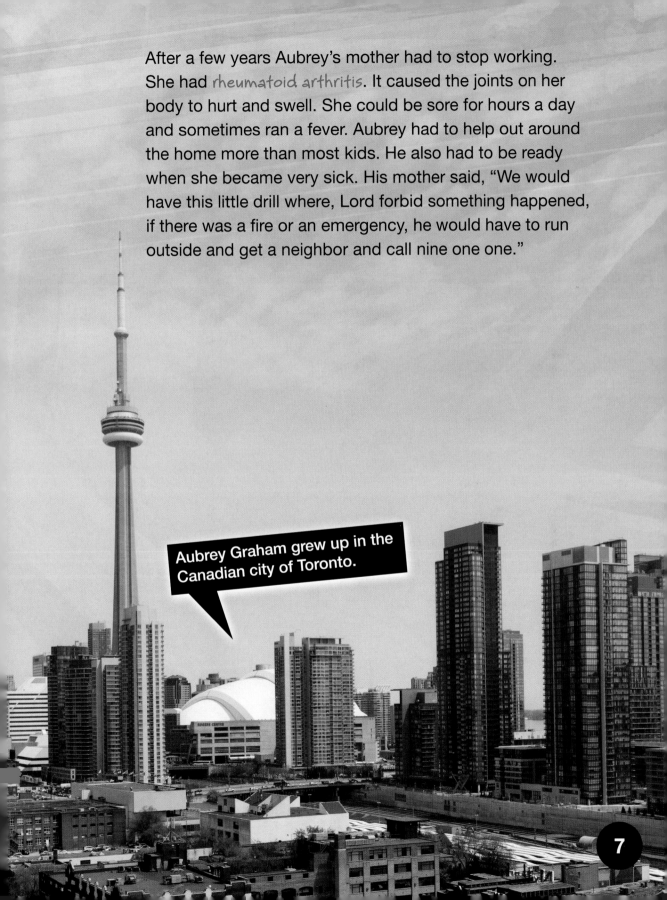

After a few years Aubrey's mother had to stop working. She had rheumatoid arthritis. It caused the joints on her body to hurt and swell. She could be sore for hours a day and sometimes ran a fever. Aubrey had to help out around the home more than most kids. He also had to be ready when she became very sick. His mother said, "We would have this little drill where, Lord forbid something happened, if there was a fire or an emergency, he would have to run outside and get a neighbor and call nine one one."

Aubrey Graham grew up in the Canadian city of Toronto.

His mother's illness drew mother and son close. Aubrey said, "I had to become a man very quickly and be the backbone for a woman who I love with all my heart, my mother." But when she was feeling well, she also tried to make life fun for her son. They celebrated Jewish holidays together. During Hanukkah she would try to make the celebrations memorable. She cooked latkes and gave him special gifts.

Aubrey and his mother also celebrated his bar mitzvah when he turned thirteen. He participated in a ceremony at his temple to show that he was old enough to obey the Jewish commandments. After the temple service, he celebrated at an Italian restaurant, listening to the Backstreet Boys.

Aubrey's mother sent him to an affluent Jewish high school. The school had an excellent reputation, but it was not easy for Aubrey. He was the only black student in the entire school. He learned to deal with being different. "Nobody understood what it was like to be black and Jewish," Aubrey said. But "being different from everyone else just made me a lot stronger."

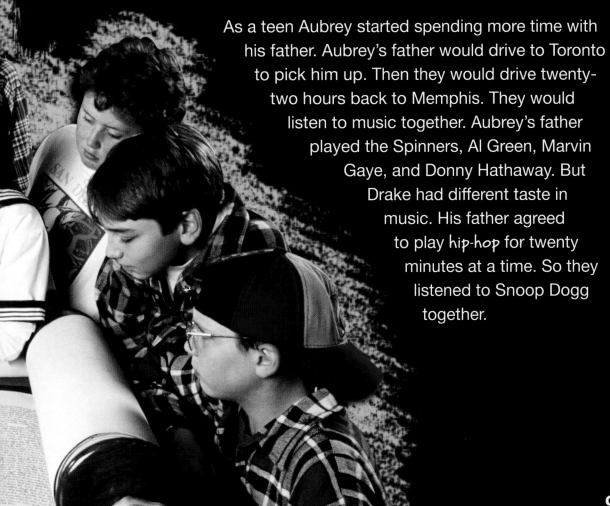

As a teen Aubrey started spending more time with his father. Aubrey's father would drive to Toronto to pick him up. Then they would drive twenty-two hours back to Memphis. They would listen to music together. Aubrey's father played the Spinners, Al Green, Marvin Gaye, and Donny Hathaway. But Drake had different taste in music. His father agreed to play hip-hop for twenty minutes at a time. So they listened to Snoop Dogg together.

In high school Aubrey was quite a class clown. He remembered, "I used to always crack jokes in class. I was a good liar and a good talker." This may not have impressed his teachers, but his classmates noticed. A boy in his class talked to him about it one day. The boy said, "Yo, my dad is an agent. You should go talk to him because you're good and you make people laugh."

Aubrey contacted his classmate's father. Then he auditioned for him. The man became Aubrey's agent. He had Aubrey take acting classes. Aubrey also started performing in plays at Toronto's Young People's Theater. Soon he was cast in commercials for Sears and General Motors Company.

In 2001 Aubrey auditioned for a Canadian teen soap opera, *Degrassi: The Next Generation*. The show was a spin-off of the other popular Degrassi series, *Degrassi High*. He landed the role of Jimmy Brooks, a wealthy young man who plays basketball for the school team. The show was one of Canada's most popular television shows. At first the series was just shown in Canada. But soon it reached American audiences on TeenNick and MTV. Eventually *Degrassi: The Next Generation* was shown in over 140 countries. This gave Aubrey a huge fan following.

The television show filmed during the school year, so Aubrey had summers off. He visited his father in Memphis. A cousin there introduced him to the southern style of rap. He also met the hip-hop artist Yo Gotti. The time with his father helped spur his interest in music.

Aubrey joined the cast of *Degrassi: The Next Generation.*

Soap Opera Star

Degrassi: The Next Generation won a number of awards. Some of them came from Canadian entertainment groups. Others came from international organizations. The cast was honored in 2002 with a Young Artist Award for Best Ensemble in a TV Series. The show also was recognized for dealing with real issues that teens faced. Stories included drug use, gangs, child abuse, and teen pregnancy.

Aubrey got a shocking storyline in the show. In the fourth season, his character Jimmy was a victim of a school shooting. Jimmy could no longer walk, so Aubrey had to learn about being handicapped. Aubrey researched for the part. He recalled, "Initially, when I found that I was going to be shot and end up in a wheel chair, I spent time with a wonderful kid who was shot and paralyzed. We went places in public, and I just wanted to see how people treat you when you're in a wheelchair." Aubrey could relate to feeling different. He simply remembered what it was like to be the only black student in his school.

At first Aubrey's character changed from being athletic to being an artist. But then the writers of *Degrassi* wanted Jimmy to rap. Aubrey was against it. He said, "I was really apprehensive about it because this is my whole leap from this and now you're going to make me into a rapper character? So I wrote my own verses and tried to keep it as not-corny as possible. And it worked out."

MENU

Aubrey's character became handicapped in the fourth season.

Aubrey became more comfortable rapping on the show. He remembered, "I was listening to the song [for Degrassi] the other day, and I was like, wow, this isn't half bad for a song on a TV show. Yeah, the music thing is definitely a big, big deal for me." In a magazine interview, Aubrey hinted at how important music was. When he was asked who he would like to change places with for a day, his answer was Jay-Z.

Aubrey worked on music away from the show too. He started writing music using his middle name, Drake. This would keep record producers and DJs from thinking that he was an actor who thought he could sing. He would have a music career that he started from scratch.

Drake's family encouraged him. He was also motivated by their success. His father's brother Larry was playing guitar for The Artist Formerly Known as Prince. Drake's dad was still playing drums when he was not in jail. Even when his father was in prison, Drake shared his songs with him. Drake would rap for his father over the phone. The other prisoners in the jail enjoyed listening to Drake as much as his father did.

Drake had even more musical talent in his family. Another uncle, Teenie Hodges, was a very well-known guitar player. He was also a very successful songwriter. He worked with soul singer Al Green on two of his biggest hits, "Take Me to the River" and "Love and Happiness." Drake knew how important his family's support was. He said, "I have a history of music and soul inside me."

Drake has many musical relatives, including his uncle, Teenie Hodges.

Drake released his first mixtape, *Room for Improvement*, in 2006. He had to borrow money from his family to make the record. Once it was done, he set up a website where people could download it. He also posted it on his MySpace page.

Fans downloaded 6,000 copies of the mixtape. It was not a huge hit. But because he did not have a record company helping advertise his music, this was still considered a small success. Fans of his music liked that he was willing to rap about his emotions. He was also clean-cut. They called him the new Fresh Prince. It gave Drake the motivation to keep writing and rapping.

Critics said that Drake had swagger, but his rap was not as hard as other artists. He was called out because he did not come from the streets. Drake responded, "I saw my dad get arrested by like a SWAT team at the border for trying to cross over. I've seen things that didn't make me happy. They were character building. That's why I think people in the hood can still connect with what I'm saying even though I'm not saying 'Yeah I got crack in my pocket' 'cause that wasn't my struggle necessarily."

Drake also started living and spending like a rich rap star when he was not. He used the money he earned from *Degrassi*. He also borrowed more from his family. He leased a Rolls Royce and drove it around Toronto. But he lived in an apartment that didn't even have a garage. So when he came home at night, he had to park his luxury car on the street.

Drake released *Room for Improvement* in 2006.

A Rap Hit

Drake kept up with his work on *Degrassi: The Next Generation*. At the same time, he was writing and recording more music. He released his second mixtape, *Comeback Season*, in 2007. Drake worked with better-known producers, including Trey Songz. Songz also rapped on three of the songs on the tape.

Comeback Season also included Drake's first single, "Replacement Girl." He even made a music video to go with the song. DJs played it in clubs, and it caught the attention of the people at BET. Their hip-hop television show, *106 & Park*, featured "Replacement Girl" as the New Joint of the Day. In other words, this was a new song worth listening to. Drake was the first Canadian rapper to be featured on *106 & Park* without a contract with a record company. BET appeared all over North America. His first mixtape was popular in Canada. But thanks to *106 & Park* he had a growing fan base in the United States as well.

The mixtape included remixes of music by Flo Rida, Kanye West, and Lil Wayne. These remixes used the original songs in the background. Drake rapped new lyrics over the recording. His producers added new instruments to the songs as well. Because mixtapes were not sold, Drake did not get in trouble for using someone else's music. He would only have to get permission and pay fees if he were selling the mixtapes. But remixing someone else's song gave Drake's fans a chance to compare his style to these other rappers.

Trey Songz and Drake worked together on *Comeback Season*.

Drake was building a reputation as a rap artist, but he was making little money at it. Mixtapes did not earn him money because they were free. He could make a little money appearing at clubs. But he was not famous enough to go on tour. He needed to keep acting on *Degrassi* to support himself.

He showed up at the television studio in 2008, ready to start filming a new season. Drake remembered, "We came in and all the names were just changed on the dressing rooms. Everyone got cut. We go upstairs and it's like, 'Who are all these people auditioning in the front?' " Drake and the entire cast had been fired.

Drake was stunned. He had to figure out how he would pay for his apartment and the payment on his car. Just as he was about to give up, he got a phone call from Houston. His friend was working with rapper Lil Wayne. Drake's friend put *Comeback Season* in Lil Wayne's CD player. After just a few minutes of listening, Lil Wayne wanted to talk to Drake. Drake remembered, "He got through like two and a half songs and stopped the CD and called me right away. Like, 'Yo, what are you doing? This is Weezy.' I was like, 'I'm just getting my hair cut.' And he said, 'I need you on a flight tonight.' "

Drake joined Lil Wayne's tour for a week. On their last night together, they recorded three songs. Drake became part of Wayne's crew called Young Money.

Drake joined Lil Wayne on tour.

With the support of Lil Wayne, Drake made another mixtape. *So Far Gone* came out in February 2009. Lil Wayne gave Drake a lot of advice in terms of writing. Drake recalled, "Wayne told me to just remember it's about your thoughts, you got to think about what you want to say beforehand … I think he gave me that advice truly for me to set myself apart as a rapper." Drake rapped about his life, including his relationships and his music career.

So Far Gone had songs with Lil Wayne, Omarion, Trey Songz, Bun B, and Lloyd. Just like his earlier tapes, it was available for free on Drake's website. His first mixtape had about 6,000 downloads in all. *So Far Gone* had two thousand downloads in just the first two hours.

Drake's music became popular with DJs in hip-hop clubs. They played so much of his music that radio stations noticed. They started playing songs from *So Far Gone*. With the large amount of radio play, the first single, "Best I Ever Had," made it to number two on the *Billboard* Hot 100. Drake also appeared on a Young Money record "Every Girl" that made it to the top ten on the *Billboard* Hot 100. Drake was only the second artist to have his first two hits in the *Billboard* top ten in one week. His second single, "Successful," reached number seventeen on the same list. With two hit singles, MTV named *So Far Gone* "The Hottest Mixtape of 2009."

Drake had his first hit single with "Best I Ever Had."

23

Selling Music

After *So Far Gone* was released, Drake performed in clubs and small concert halls. He appeared with Lil Wayne and the Young Money Entertainment artists. He also performed with other rappers at clubs. Fans were eager for him to release his first album.

Before he had a chance to sell his first album, someone else did. Canadian Money Entertainment put an album called *The Girls Love Drake* up for sale on iTunes, Rhapsody, and Amazon. It had songs from *So Far Gone* and some of his earlier releases. People were so excited to finally buy music from Drake that it would have debuted at 101 on the *Billboard* album chart.

Drake performs with Young Jeezy in concert.

Drake and his manager discovered that Canadian Money Entertainment was selling his mixtape music. This created a huge problem for Drake. Some of the songs on *The Girls Love Drake* used beats and samples from other artists' songs. On the free mixtapes that was not a problem. Since Drake did not make money from the mixtape, he did not owe the artists money for using their samples. But he could not sell these songs without getting the artists' permission first. Canadian Money Entertainment made it look like Drake was using the samples without permission. Drake could be sued by every artist that he sampled on the songs.

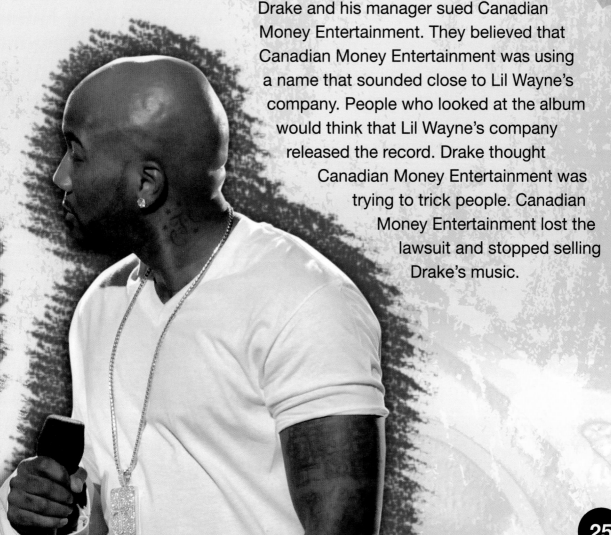

Drake and his manager sued Canadian Money Entertainment. They believed that Canadian Money Entertainment was using a name that sounded close to Lil Wayne's company. People who looked at the album would think that Lil Wayne's company released the record. Drake thought Canadian Money Entertainment was trying to trick people. Canadian Money Entertainment lost the lawsuit and stopped selling Drake's music.

The popularity of *So Far Gone* made Drake even more famous. Other hip-hop artists noticed that he could write, sing, and rap. Mary J. Blige, Jay-Z, Kanye West, Timbaland, Jamie Foxx, and Eminem all had Drake on their albums.

It was unusual for an artist to have two singles make the Hot 100 chart without a record company helping sell them. This meant that the record company would not have to take a risk on an unknown artist. Drake was proven. He was already able to make money on his music. Many record companies offered Drake contracts.

Finally Drake made a deal in June 2009. Universal Motown and Lil Wayne's Young Money Entertainment would work together with Drake. The deal was amazing. Drake was paid over one million dollars just for negotiating with Universal Motown. He also kept the rights to the masters for his future records. In other words, any time his music was used by someone in the future, he would get paid for it. He would not have to share those profits. He could also say no to anyone wanting to use his music. Few artists have control over their masters like this. Because Drake was a new artist, this level of control was unheard of.

Universal Motown and Young Money knew they could make money on Drake's older music. They rereleased five of the songs from *So Far Gone* as an EP. It reached number six on *Billboard* Top 200 album chart. It sold over half a million copies. And at the Juno Awards, it won Rap Recording of the Year.

Eminem and Drake rapped together for a song on Eminem's album.

Touring and Recording

Drake went on his first major tour. The "America's Most Wanted" tour included Lil Wayne, Soulja Boy, and Young Jeezy. Drake rapped "Best I Ever Had" with Lil Wayne and performed a few of his own songs too. In the July 31, 2009, show, Drake fell and injured his knee. He had to have surgery and get physical therapy before he could go back on tour.

The Grammy Award nominations came out at the end of 2009. Drake was nominated for two Grammys for his single, "Best I Ever Had" from the *So Far Gone* EP. He was also invited to perform at the Grammy Awards ceremony. He rapped with Lil Wayne and Eminem at the very end of the show. They rapped two songs that they had never performed live before.

In the same month as the Grammys, a massive earthquake struck Haiti. Over 300,000 people were killed. Over one million Haitians were left homeless. Canadian recording artists agreed to put out a record and give the money raised to help the Haitian survivors. They called themselves Young Artists for Haiti. Drake sang a solo verse on the song "Wavin' Flag."

Drake was supposed to release his first full album in the fall of 2009. Then his record company announced they would release it in March 2010. They delayed it again, announcing that it would come out on May 25. Finally, on June 15, 2010, *Thank Me Later* was released. It included performances by Lil Wayne, Alicia Keys, Nicki Minaj, and Jay-Z.

Drake and K'naan performed at the 2010 Juno Awards.

29

Drake's debut album, *Thank Me Later*, reached number one on the *Billboard* Top 200 the week it came out. It topped the Canadian record charts too. He released four singles from the album. The lead single, "Over," reached number fourteen on the *Billboard* Hot 100. His second single, "Find Your Love," reached number eight. "Miss Me," the third single, reached number fifteen. "Fancy," the fourth single, reached number twenty-five.

On the day the album finally came out, Drake was all over New York City. He had many fans who were thrilled to buy the album and listen to Drake's new songs. He appeared at a Best Buy store to sign copies of his album. Crowds lined up to have a chance to say hello. Then Drake spent hours on the phone. He gave interviews to radio stations. The disc jockeys let fans know that Drake was giving a free concert with the band Hanson at the South Seaport in New York City that evening.

The concert area at the seaport could hold about 10,000 people. Young fans were excited to see the handsome brothers in Hanson. They had a huge hit with the song "Mmmm-bop" in 1997. But kids who had loved *Degrassi's* Jimmy Brooks and listened to Drake on the radio were thrilled to see him live. So instead of 10,000 fans, over 20,000 showed up.

Some fans closest to the stage were getting crushed. So some people started pushing. Others threw punches. Shortly after Hansen started to sing, police broke up the show. Six people suffered minor injuries. Disappointed fans never saw Drake perform.

With his album a hit, the next step would be for Drake to go on a tour of his own. He called it "The Away from Home Tour." Drake visited twenty-five cities across the United States in just over a month. The tour included stops at colleges where Drake promoted "green" performances. He used Earth-friendly fuel and promoted recycling.

Drake was then scheduled to perform all over Europe. But in late June, his mother became very ill. She would need surgery. Drake decided to cancel his European tour to be with his mother. He said, "I have made the difficult decision to cancel my European tour in order to support her during her recovery, just as she supported me through the years." Drake chose his mother over the money that the tour could have made. He stayed in Toronto and helped her as she recovered.

Drake felt passionate about his ties to Canada. He knew first-hand how hard it was for Canadian hip-hop artists to get a break. So Drake helped establish Toronto's October's Very Own Festival. It was Toronto's first major hip-hop concert festival. In October 2010 the festival featured major stars, including Jay-Z, Eminem, Rick Ross, Young Jeezy, Bun B, and Fabolous.

The festival also gave Toronto rappers a chance to shine. Drake was a big fan of The Weeknd after hearing his mixtape. Drake remembered, "The Weeknd was presented to me, and anybody with any form of an ear can understand why I had to fully embrace that." Just like Lil Wayne gave Drake his first big break, Drake did the same for The Weeknd.

33

Breaking a Mold

Drake stood out among most other hip-hop stars. He did not come from the United States. Drake was a soap opera actor. He never sold drugs or struggled with poverty. And, of course, he was Jewish. Just like in school, Drake was different. But he had a great attitude about it. He said, "At the end of the day, I consider myself a black man because I'm more immersed in black culture than any other. Being Jewish is kind of a cool twist. It makes me unique." Drake hoped that his uniqueness would help his career.

Being Jewish was not completely new to hip-hop. The Beastie Boys rapped about their Jewish faith. But they were also white. Many hip-hop fans did not consider the Beastie Boys rappers because they started as a punk band. They were outsiders without considering their faith.

This did not mean that there were few Jews in hip-hop. They were behind the scenes. Many record company executives were Jewish. So were lawyers that worked on contracts. Rappers even called out their Jewish jewelers when they sang about their bling.

Drake is open about his religion. He wears Jewish symbols. He mentions his faith in interviews and lyrics. Jewish fans can identify with Drake. Fans who are not Jewish can become more familiar and comfortable with it.

Some faithful Jews worry about other messages in Drake's music and videos. His music uses profanity, as many hip-hop songs do. Drake also sings about sex. His videos often show women in skimpy clothes. These things do not agree with Jewish teaching.

Drake is open about his Jewish faith.

Drake does not fit the hip-hop stereotype in other ways. He dresses in a very preppy style. He does not sport many tattoos. He looks like a kid from the suburbs, not a hard-living rap artist. Other rappers have called him out on it. Pusha T called Drake out in a song, saying that Drake's sweaters did not match his swagger. Drake responded, "It's funny because people only talk about me and sweaters because I don't give them anything else to talk about."

Another criticism that Drake often hears is that his music is too "emo." Very few hip-hop songs deal with feelings and emotions. Drake does not mind expressing himself. He explained, "I wish that we lived in a time and a generation where people would stop viewing my honesty as overly emotional." He also does not think that rapping about emotions makes him look weak. He said, "People always act like I spend my life crying in a dark room. I don't, I'm good. I'm a man."

Hip-hop music is full of diss records. Artists insult each other in their rhymes. Sometimes the feuds get nasty. But Drake tries to stay above the bad feelings. He said, "If someone wants to bring a problem to me, it's strictly based on their immense amount of hate for me. It's never because I've sparked that using my voice, my image, or my outlet. I never use my outlet for confrontation or negativity, ever. I always try and give people music to ride to and music to enjoy. All I ever ask in return is that it's mutual love."

Drake says he never acts in a negative way. But he has been in feuds.

Common is a rapper from Chicago. In one of his raps, he said that Drake's music had turned hip-hop soft.

Rick Ross put out a record that featured Drake, "Stay Schemin." In one verse Drake rapped that some people attacked him just to sell more records. He did not mention Common by name. But fans knew who he was talking about. Common made a remix of "Stay Schemin" just days after the song came out. In it he called Drake "Canada Dry." He also challenged Drake to be brave enough to diss Common by name.

Drake never answered Common, but he got back at him another way. Common had a long relationship with champion tennis player Serena Williams. After they broke up, Serena dated Drake. They went on vacation together. He sent tweets that showed they were together. He even thanked her by name in the notes of his second album, *Take Care*. He wrote, "You have given me a very exciting year, and I am so grateful to have you in my life …"

Common is not the only rapper who has had a beef with Drake. Chris Brown dated the singer Rihanna. They broke up when he beat her up. Then Drake and Rihanna dated. One evening, Drake, Chris Brown, and both stars' *entourages* were in the same club. A huge fight broke out. Chris Brown was cut by a champagne bottle. Drake said he did not fight. Days later, Brown released a diss track. He said Drake was scared.

Serena Williams dated Common before Drake had a relationship with her.

Life Away from Music

Some celebrities keep their personal lives private. Drake shares his life in his music. So fans hear him sing about his love life. They also see him in photos in *tabloids*.

In his teens Drake dated Keshia Chanté. She is a Canadian singer and actress. In his song "Deceiving," he rapped about their relationship. He did a remix of one of her songs, changing the words to talk about their romance. He mentioned how much they had grown. He also said that he still loved her. In an interview he said, "Would I call Keshia Chanté an ex? I'd be proud to say she is an ex. I'm proud to say we had our time, when we were, like 16 years old. She's great. She's one of the first people in the industry that I met, we just connected."

Drake's romance with Rihanna was up and down. For a while, she told the press that they were just friends. Drake felt like she used him to get over Chris Brown. He said, "I don't even know if I wrote a rap song in that whole nine months, because I wasn't a rapper anymore. I didn't believe in myself. I was someone else's property. I was a pawn. You know what she was doing to me? She was doing exactly what I've done to so many women throughout my life, which is show them quality time, then disappear. I was like, 'wow, this feels terrible."

He has a very close relationship with fellow Young Money artist Nicki Minaj. He said, "We have the most interesting relationship, 'cause it's so multilayered. That's my co-worker, my peer, my family. But, at the same time, on any given day, she's, like, the love of my life."

Drake and Nicki Minaj are very close.

41

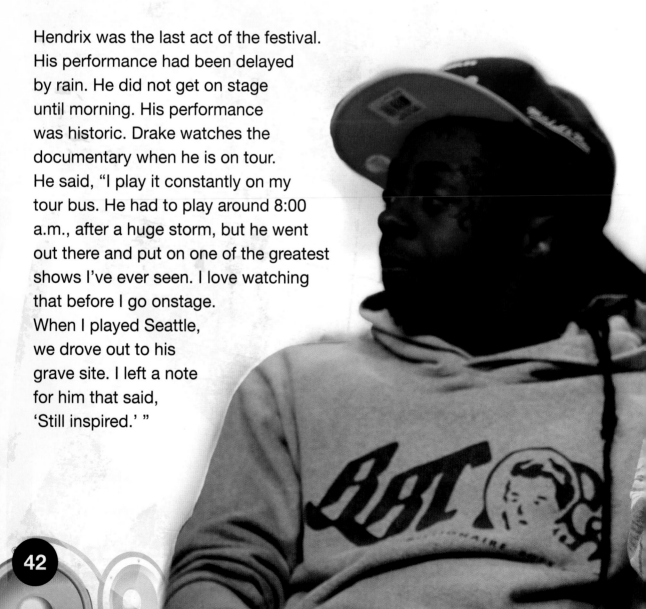

Drake has worked with many artists. He shared music with his father driving to and from Memphis. But Drake also found inspiration in a musician who died before Drake was ever born.

Jimi Hendrix was one of the best electric guitar players of all time. In the late 1960s, he helped move people's taste in music from folk to rock. Hendrix was invited to the Woodstock Music Festival in 1969. Filmmakers made a documentary about the show.

Hendrix was the last act of the festival. His performance had been delayed by rain. He did not get on stage until morning. His performance was historic. Drake watches the documentary when he is on tour. He said, "I play it constantly on my tour bus. He had to play around 8:00 a.m., after a huge storm, but he went out there and put on one of the greatest shows I've ever seen. I love watching that before I go onstage. When I played Seattle, we drove out to his grave site. I left a note for him that said, 'Still inspired.' "

Drake is also still inspired by his friend Lil Wayne. In 2010 Lil Wayne went to prison for having a gun and drugs. Lil Wayne rapped over the phone for a song Drake recorded. When Drake visited, Lil Wayne encouraged him to be true to himself. Drake remembered Lil Wayne saying, " 'Don't change yourself, please. You got it. I've never met a young dude that has it figured out, but you got it. Don't mess it up. Just be you. Sing! Rap! Be you. Don't stop smiling.' That's what he said."

Drake and Lil Wayne enjoy a basketball game together.

Drake has developed work outside of music. He has returned to acting. He provided the voice of Ethan in *Ice Age: Continental Drift*. He also had lead roles in two short films. Drake also made commercials for Sprite. The commercial had a prime airing spot, right before the Superbowl. Kodak hired Drake to represent the company for an ad campaign. They developed a camera that can send photos straight to Facebook and Twitter. Stars like Drake will help Kodak sell the new camera to young shoppers. Virgin Airlines painted Drake's face on the side of one of their airplanes, calling it Air Drake. The plane flies from Toronto to cities in California. Virgin used Drake as an ambassador for Toronto.

Drake has also invested money in real estate. He purchased two condos in Miami. They were side-by-side units in the same building. He tore down walls and made it one huge apartment. Drake used the remodeled apartment in his video "I'm On One." Then he sold the apartment for more money than he paid for them. Next he bought a mansion in Los Angeles that was valued at nine million dollars.

In 2011 Drake was ranked at number eleven on *Forbes* magazine's "Cash Kings" list. The Cash Kings are the people in hip-hop who made the most money over the previous year. Drake earned $11 million. Just three years earlier, he was worried about paying for the lease on his car. Now he was making more money than most other hip-hop artists.

Drake has just two albums in his young career. MTV ranked him the second-hottest MC in rap music in 2012. Only his friend Rick Ross came out ahead of him. He has had twelve songs on *Billboard's* Rap Chart at once. He has had songs at number one, two, and three on the Rap Chart at the same time. With a new album in the works, Drake is prepared to become an even bigger force in hip-hop.

Drake made commercials for Kodak cameras.

Vocabulary

affluent	(adjective)	wealthy
agent	(noun)	a person who finds work for a performer
audition	(verb)	to try out for something; to perform for a show or an agent
bar mitzvah	(noun)	a celebration of a Jewish boy's coming of age
Billboard	(noun)	magazine that covers the music industry, including record and album sales
campaign	(noun)	organized work or an organized plan
contract	(noun)	an agreement between two people, between two companies, or between a person and a company
debut	(verb)	to make a first appearance
diss	(adjective)	insulting
emo	(adjective)	emotional
ensemble	(noun)	a group of people who perform together
entourage	(noun)	the people who surround an important person
EP	(noun)	an extended play recording, usually longer than a single but shorter than an album
feud	(noun)	a fight that lasts over a long time
Grammy Award	(noun)	an award given to the best U.S. recording artists every year by The Recording Academy
Hanukkah	(noun)	an eight-day Jewish holiday, called the Festival of Lights

hip-hop	(adjective or noun)	music that uses strong beats and chanted words
inspiration	(noun)	someone or something that motivates or spurs on
Juno Awards	(noun)	awards given to the best Canadian recording artists every year
latke	(noun)	a potato pancake, traditionally served at Jewish holidays
lease	(verb)	to rent
manager	(noun)	a person who does business on someone's behalf, a representative
master	(noun)	the original of a recording that copies can be made from
mixtape	(noun)	a CD of songs made without a record company
negotiate	(verb)	to bargain or haggle in order to make a deal
producer	(noun)	a person who raises money to create a song, a stage show, and so on
profanity	(noun)	swearing or other inappropriate language
promote	(verb)	to sell or advertise for a product
rap	(verb)	to speak with rhythm along with music
rheumatoid arthritis	(noun)	a disorder that attacks the joints, causing pain, swelling, stiffness, and fever
sample	(noun or verb)	to take parts of songs and combine them with new music
single	(noun)	one song, usually from an album
tabloid	(noun)	gossip magazines and websites
undependable	(adjective)	not reliable

Photo Credits